A SPIRIT DAUGHTER WORKBOOK

WRITTEN BY
JILL WINTERSTEEN

FOR THE FULL MOON

THURSDAY, JANUARY 25TH, 2024

9:55 AM PT

WHY THE FULL MOON

The Full Moon represents the peak of the lunar cycle. It is when the work we've done since the New Moon culminates and our intentions manifest, or when we realize where those intentions are blocked. The Full Moon is a time of both celebration and revelation, when we can honor the steps we have made and see what in our lives needs attention to shift. Full Moons feel intense to the energetic body. They stir up emotions, both consciously and subconsciously. Although their intensity can feel challenging to our systems, it is ultimately a good thing. Every Full Moon provides us the opportunity to transform our emotions and raise our vibration one Moon at a time.

WHY THE FULL MOON

To work with the emotions revealed by the Full Moon, we must be willing to feel them. We need to lean into them and allow ourselves to understand their origins. Of course, we always have free will and can choose to ignore what rises to the surface. This suppression, though, tends to lead to sleepless nights, irritability, and even physical ailments around the Full Moon. What we resist really does persist. Our true essence, which is beneath our emotions, wants to feel  good. We want to resolve our negative emotions, and we want to heal. The Full Moon amplifies our desire to work through the feelings that block us from living our best lives. It reminds us that life is to be celebrated. We are capable and worthy of feeling joy, gratitude, and love. Furthermore, these energies are well within our reach if we are willing to work through the blocks that prevent the full manifestation of our intentions.

At the deepest layers of our physical bodies, we are energetic beings made of subtle frequencies. We are not that much different from light or sound, as we consist of waves vibrating at different levels. Depending on our thoughts and emotions, we vibrate at higher or lower frequencies. Your overall vibration is created by the many thoughts and emotions running through your body at any one time. One thought or emotion, though, can take over your entire vibration and affect all areas of your life—even the ones you think are not connected. For instance, if you feel frustrated by a situation at work, your overall vibration lowers as a result. This lower vibration disrupts other parts of your life, including your relationships and your health, and even your ability to see beauty in the world. It can also block your potential to manifest your intentions. When we exist in a higher vibratory state, aligned with love, gratitude, passion, and joy, we find ourselves in the flow. We attract everything we need to help us manifest our highest visions and our greatest potential. Things magically fall into place with little effort. Abundance becomes available to us, and we feel an overwhelming sense of appreciation for everything in our lives—even our challenges.

The Full Moon brings us the opportunity to vibrate at a higher level by shedding light on what lowers our vibrations. With the help of the Moon, we can see thoughts, feelings, and even words we use to block ourselves from attracting the lives of our dreams. We are already connected to everything we desire. The reality we want to live is possible and, in many ways, is already available to us if we are willing to let go of anything that prevents us from living it. The Full Moon is the time to become aware of and release any energy that prevents us from manifesting our visions. Through conscious effort and attention, we can shift energies we no longer want to carry and welcome energies that align with our souls.

We celebrate each Full Moon and remember the magic of the Universe we live in. Full Moons are important times of the lunar cycle that remind us of the infinite space we are a part of, its mystery, and its power. No matter what this Full Moon brings, feel joy for your life and celebrate this time. Remember, you are made of the same energy that the Universe around you is made of. You are the Moon, the ocean, and the planets. You are just as powerful, magical, and beautiful. Feel into the truth of your power and honor it as you honor the Full Moon.

LEO FULL MOON

The first Full Moon of 2024 occurs in Leo, greeting us at the start of Aquarius Season. While Aquarius teaches us to shift the collective consciousness by being ourselves, Leo helps us decide what that means. Leo represents our center. Ruled by the Sun, this sign reminds us of what holds us together. It helps us feel our truth, and more importantly, it helps us feel our hearts. This Moon can help your break through all the layers placed upon you that dim your light. It helps you find yourself, what you love, and what you ultimately want to express to the world. The Leo Full Moon is the time to find what makes you shine your brightest and embrace that part of yourself despite any fear of rejection. Instead, the Leo Full Moon teaches you to love yourself fiercely and let love change the world.

Leo is the regal lion of the zodiac. It embodies the energies of leadership, compassion, vulnerability, strength, and love. With Leo's energy governing the Full Moon, we are encouraged to focus on the heart's truth. Acknowledging this takes courage and vulnerability. It's not always easy to listen to and follow our hearts. Our mind often has different plans and will try to convince us these plans are safer. This Full Moon, though, is the time to listen to the heart and follow its lead, even if we are unsure of the road ahead. It's a time to feel the guidance of the heart through our emotions and let it give us the answers we've been looking for all along.

Aquarius Season teaches us that we are energy and have an energetic field with a corresponding frequency. Leo reminds us that the heart is the center of our energetic field and emits an electromagnetic frequency greater than any other part of us. The heart's energetic field extends far past our bodies and influences others around us through its frequency. The heart is powerful, and this Full Moon reminds us to tend to it and ensure that it is sending out the vibrations that accurately represent who we are at our cores. If our hearts are our energetic messengers to the world, then this is the time to clarify the heart's expression and raise its vibration.

Part of tending to the heart is listening to it. Following it, though, can make us feel vulnerable. The heart does not come with organized spreadsheets that tell us the exact trajectory of our decisions. The heart is messy, complicated, and may feel illogical at times. It contains all of our feelings, including our pain, regret, and

LEO FULL MOON

fear. It also holds our joy, love, compassion, and gratitude. To feel and amplify the positive vibrations of the heart, we must also be willing to feel and understand everything else the heart holds. We cannot open our hearts and feel only the good things. We have to stand in the presence of all of it, which can make us feel scared, vulnerable, and even ashamed. Leo teaches us, though, to show up for ourselves with courage and strength. It reminds us that we can face anything within ourselves with love and compassion. It also teaches us that the pathway to leading from the heart starts by understanding its full depths.

Over this Full Moon, find some time to sit with yourself and listen to your heart. Feel what you've avoided or shut down in your heart. Ask your heart what it wants to tell you and be open to learning from it. Breathe into your heart and listen to it without the mind and its thoughts interfering. We often think the mind is the center of our beings, but it's not. The mind would like to trick us into thinking it is in control, but the heart is the one that leads us forward. The heart knows the direction we must travel to align with life's purpose, and the heart knows how to tap into the infinite wisdom of the Universe. The mind is simply along for the ride.

There is always inner-child work available to us on the Leo Full Moon. Leo is associated with the energy of play and children. It brings out our wounds around love, approval, and courage created in childhood. Align with this Full Moon to have a conversation with your inner child and ask them what they need to feel loved. Let them know they are accepted and loved for simply being themselves. Align with Leo to play with some of these concepts and hold space for your inner child to reveal themselves. Reflect on how you were taught to love and be loved. Also, notice if your inner child associates love with approval from others. Do you feel you need to do something to earn love? Or is love freely given to you? Do you feel you deserve love simply for being yourself? Take some time to heal your inner child and give them love this Full Moon.

Whether you received unconditional love or not as a child, you can give it to yourself now. The Leo Full Moon is the perfect time to begin developing love for yourself without conditions. It begins by loving yourself for being you. You do not need to do anything, accomplish anything, or create anything to be loved. You deserve unconditional love for merely existing. Feel into this energy of love throughout the Full Moon. Write yourself a love letter today and remind yourself of your inherent beauty and perfection. Align with Leo to know you are worthy of love, always, and allow this love to bring out your true essence.

Leo reminds us that we all are unique in our own way. Each of us has a unique set of talents, which need to be honored and shared with those around us. Each of us also has a message that comes from the heart. The Leo Full Moon is a time to find your heart's message and send it to the world. Leo is the sign of kings and queens. It reminds us that each of us has the potential to lead others through the full expression of ourselves. We must, though, be willing to be seen. Kings and queens are generally the center of attention in any room. They feel confident enough to take up that space. From this platform they can lead and share their energy. Feel into your own willingness to take up the space you deserve this Full Moon, and use it to share your heart's gifts with others. Express your heart and allow its messages to extend far past the confines of your body. Accept and love yourself for who you are this Full Moon and let that love allow you to shine your brightest light into the world.

LEO MOON X AQUARIUS SUN

On the Leo Full Moon, we are working with the energies of Leo and Aquarius, where the Sun is positioned. Leo and Aquarius oppose each other in the sky and differ energetically in many ways. But they also have many similarities. This Full Moon is an opportunity to find their common ground and harness their combined energy to help you create the breakthroughs needed to step into your heart and your highest Self.

Astrological energies, like emotions, have a lower and a higher vibration. Think of each zodiac sign as a spectrum of frequencies. We align with a particular zodiac frequency at different points of our lives and take on its resulting qualities in mind, body, and spirit. Leo's higher frequencies include the qualities of a benevolent leader. Leo aligns us with the vibrations of courage, compassion, empathy, and honor. When we tune in to this high side of Leo, we hear the messages of our hearts without judgment. We listen with only unconditional love. We wholeheartedly love and accept every aspect of ourselves. Furthermore, we express ourselves fully to the world without fear of rejection. In this high state of Leo, we embody the confidence and poise of a great leader who accepts approval but does not depend upon it. We find our highest Self and share that person with the world, unrestricted by the ego.

When working with the vibrations of Leo, we come up against the ego, which is Leo's shadow. The ego is the part of us that yearns to be defined by something. It is how we identify ourselves, including the conditioned patterns we have formed about who we are in this life. It is also our inner critic, our self-defeating thoughts, and the part of us that feels separated from others. The ego can get in the way of us finding and expressing our true selves. It attaches to ideas of how we "should" behave in the world and how others "should" receive us. The ego's fuel is fear, and it can often lead us down dark paths of needing constant validation and approval of what we express to the world. The ego's role should be to motivate us, remind us of our purpose when needed, and help us function in society. But it should not lead our lives. On this Full Moon, we have the opportunity to recognize when the ego has taken the reins and, in its effort to define our existence, closed the full expression of the heart.

The counterpart to the ego is the higher Self. When we align with Leo's and Aquarius's highest vibrations, we tap into our highest Selves and the higher consciousness of love. This highest Self is the part of us that is connected to the entire energy of the Universe and, therefore, to everyone and everything around us.

LEO MOON X AQUARIUS SUN

When moving from the higher self, there is no need to compare or compete with others because we are all one. Without separation, we do not feel insecurity, lack, or unworthiness. When we operate from the higher Self, we are always connected to the heart's message. We do not need to distract ourselves from our feelings, for we understand that the true nature of ourselves is pure love and beauty. From this place, we feel fulfilled in our lives and are confident in everything we do because we are constantly moving from the heart. We no longer worry about rejection or approval from others. We feel confident in who we are. To remain centered within the higher Self, we need to be deeply aware of when the ego takes over, then redirect our energy toward higher vibrations of compassion, love, and connection. Aligning with the higher Self allows us to honor our true essence—the heart—and give its message freely to the collective without needing approval.

As we work with this Full Moon's energy, we have the opportunity to connect with our higher Selves. This opportunity is the true merger of Leo, Aquarius, and their corresponding frequencies. Throughout this Full Moon, ask yourself how you might be aligned with the lower vibration of each sign. When we align with Leo's shadow side, we become demanding, need approval, and feel insecure. We seek external validation instead of feeling our power. We can even cause drama in our lives and the lives of others to gain the attention we need to feel secure within ourselves. This lower vibration of Leo disconnects us from our hearts. Instead, it aligns us with the delusions of the ego. We latch on to our identities and forget that we are beings made of pure love, capable of deep compassion and unlimited joy. Spend some time this Full Moon thinking about where you may be aligning with these vibrations of Leo. Resist the urge to judge yourself. Judgment can drop you into an even lower vibration. Instead, accept these parts of yourself and welcome them to your conscious awareness. When you become aware of your shadow sides, you immediately form control over them, and they stop controlling you.

While you observe places where you may be aligning with Leo's shadow side, feel how you may align with Aquarius's. When we embody Aquarius's lower vibrations, we become overly judgmental and critical of others, especially those in authority positions. Instead of helping change what we do not like in the world, we complain and detach from the world. We disconnect from the vibration of love and acceptance and become aloof. We withhold our energy while acting superior to everyone around us. Notice if there are any places in your life where you may be aligning with these lower vibrations and, again without judgment, accept them. Accepting them will help you acknowledge the behavior. Through this awareness, you will shift it and find Aquarius's higher vibrations. When we step into the highest frequencies of Aquarius, we can feel the infinite connection between the Universe and us. We understand that we are just one part of a bigger collective. We want to contribute our energy to making the world a better place by connecting with the vibration of love and acceptance.

When we shift away from the lower vibrations of both Leo and Aquarius, we make space for the higher ones. We have the opportunity with this pair to vibrate to a higher level than ever before. These two energies allow us to feel the heart's messages and honor them while honoring the collective. We learn to express ourselves from a place of love and gratitude instead of a place of judgment or neediness. We embody the true age of Aquarius, in which everyone contributes their unique talents while working together for the good of everyone on the planet. Take the time this Full Moon to feel what your heart wants to give to the world and courageously create a life that embodies its message.

ASPECTS

The Leo Full Moon takes place one day before Uranus stations direct. This means Uranus, the planet of change and ruler of Aquarius, is highly active today. It also means that after tomorrow, all planets will be stationed direct until April 1st. Uranus's activation today helps you break through old patterns of the heart and ego. You may feel triggered more than usual today, or you may notice your actions more clearly. Your limiting beliefs may be amplified or illuminated somehow, bringing them to your conscious awareness. Notice emotions that surface on this Full Moon and ask if they reveal a pattern ready to break. If so, approach yourself with compassion and do the work needed to unravel and detach from energy that no longer serves who you are.

As Uranus approaches direct motion, the energy of the cosmos quickens. This period each year, when all planets are moving forward, feels fast-paced to our nervous system. Notice if you feel the need to rush or the pressure to do something in haste this Full Moon. Take a deep breath and let your decisions come from a grounded place, not one of pressure. We will have all of February and March to work with the energy of forward motion. During this time, pay close attention to your resounding yeses. It can be easy to overextend yourself during this period. Make sure whatever you say yes to, you will want to continue to say yes six months from now. Be clear about your commitments and even more precise with your focus. Keep returning to the intentions you set on the first New Moon of the year, and align with this Full Moon to say no to everything else. Remember, the New Moon helps us plant seeds, and the Full Moon helps us bring them to fruition. Some of your dreams will require strong boundaries and loud no's to manifest. Create a daily practice during this time that helps you become clear on where you are focusing your energy for the day and mantras that help you maintain this focus.

This Full Moon will also work with Jupiter in Taurus, creating a square aspect. Squares cause friction and tension until a breakthrough is reached. Jupiter is the planet of expansion, luck, and abundance. As this giant planet squares the Full Moon, you may feel resistance around areas of your life that need expansion. This Full Moon wants you to step into your brilliance. It wants you to take up the space you deserve. It wants you to claim your power. Where are you not doing those things? Again, you may feel triggered around situations that bring up your expansion or power. You may find emotions coming out of nowhere when these topics arise. Pay attention to where you feel tension in your body, energy, and emotions. There is something to learn there and a potential for a breakthrough.

The square aspect with Jupiter also illuminates ways you may limit yourself. With Leo theming this Full Moon, ego attachments are revealed. These are places in your life where you are so attached to how you are perceived or your identity definitions that you become limited. This Full Moon may show how holding onto behaviors that make you feel that you fit in with others or fit a box defined by someone else is preventing you from stepping into your highest self. Aquarius and Leo teach us that true belonging exists when we align with ourselves and attract a community that accepts us for who we are. This is also how we find authentic leadership— through being ourselves, even if it feels vulnerable. Allow this Full Moon to help you shed layers of identity you placed on yourself that prevent you from being your most authentic self. Instead, be you and attract people who accept you from that person—not the self the ego tells you to be.

Finally, we have some influence from Pluto, newly in Aquarius, this Full Moon. Pluto just entered Aquarius, setting the stage for the next two decades. The Sun sits close to this planet, and the Moon opposes it. Pluto helps us heal from the past. It helps us understand the cycles of our lives, the choices we make, and the lessons we are here to learn in this lifetime. Through this understanding, it helps us transform. Feel this planet's energy helping you shift outdated patterns that keep you attached to your pain. Instead, turn them into healing, including how to help someone else heal. Pluto guides us in turning our pain into power so that it no longer holds us back from what is meant to be ours.

As you work with the energy of Pluto in Aquarius today, ask yourself what you need to transform to claim your power. Remember, the Leo Full Moon wants you to own your power. Align with Pluto to help you transmute anything preventing you from realizing your brilliance and strength to create your life. You may not be able to change your past, but you can shape your current reality any way you desire. Decide what future you are ready to claim this Full Moon, ensure it aligns with your highest truth, and then step into it. It's time.

HOUSESCOPES

ARIES RISING
The Leo Full Moon lands in your fifth house of creativity and romance, Aries, and there could be powerful identity shifts coming into your conscious awareness. Because of an opposition with Pluto, your relationship with friends and lovers is ready to evolve. Think back to the corresponding Leo New Moon last August and consider how themes from back then are culminating. You're ready to grow and create like never before, and anyone creating drama in your community might not be able to keep up.

TAURUS RISING
The Leo Full Moon lands in your fourth house of home and family, Taurus, and all signs point to fireworks on the homefront. Of course fireworks are known for being dramatic and beautiful, but they can also be dangerous! As there's an opposition with Pluto in your tenth house of career, notice any push and pull between your work-life balance. The Leo New Moon back in August last year might highlight similar themes that have reached their breaking point. Whatever happens, know that your family life is expanding as your own faith in yourself publicly gains traction. Be on the lookout for big opportunities.

GEMINI RISING
The Leo Full Moon lands in your third house of perception, Gemini, and you might find your daily routines to be expanding in a way you hadn't previously envisioned. Because of an opposition with Pluto in your ninth house of travel and higher beliefs, a fresh perspective might be in order around this Full Moon. Let yourself get lost in the library or in a neighboring city and see what information finds you. While sometimes transporting yourself can truly lead to a rebirth, it's also true that wherever you go, there you are. Ponder how you're showing up in different environments and why.

CANCER RISING
The Leo Full Moon lands in your second house of resources, Cancer, and asks you to acknowledge the support you receive from other people. This axis of the birth chart is fundamentally about your values and self-worth, so if you're feeling challenged in this area at all, look to your friends as a loving mirror. There are ample opportunities available to you now, and the hardest part might be discernment around which will be most fruitful in the long term. Trust yourself to know where to commit your energy and it will pay dividends.

LEO RISING
The Leo Full Moon, of course, lands in your first house of self, Leo, and asks you to do what you do best: shine brightly and radiate it outward to the furthest corners of the room. No one knows how to channel energy like you do, and coupled with an opposition to Pluto in your house of partnership...that will be all the more clear in your relationships. You're undergoing an intense recalibration in this area of your life, and there may be opportunities around this date to understand some of the key themes that will be surfacing. Make note of how you're taking up space in the world and don't apologize for being your most authentic, vibrant self.

HOUSESCOPES

VIRGO RISING

The Leo Full Moon lands in your twelfth house of solitude, Virgo, and you're likely juggling the need for some rest and relaxation with your daily responsibilities. The secret, which is much less dramatic than you might imagine...is that there's room for both in your life. While your responsibilities day to day might be increasing, that doesn't negate the space required to recharge. Trust that your growth edges are supported by having your own back and answering the call for solitude when it whispers.

LIBRA RISING

The Leo Full Moon lands in your eleventh house of community, Libra, and it's an omen for both your friendships and your personal responsibility within them undergoing a major transformation. Whether people in your circle are bringing the drama, you're busy proactively addressing the concerns of your inner-child, or both at the same time... this lunation is about balancing your needs versus the collectives. Trust your need for romance around this date, too. Indulge in the many ways you can engage with creativity and trust yourself to shine that light into your connections.

SCORPIO RISING

The Leo Full Moon lands in your tenth house of career, Scorpio, and you're taking your rightful spot center stage at the office. You're familiar, though, with the concept of everything coming at a price– and this lunation might highlight the energy you're spending at work versus home. Even still, this lunation is all about the heart, and you can trust where it leads you. If there are any rebirths bubbling up on the homefront, know that your public facing decisions are led by your deep courage to spread the truth far and wide.

SAGITTARIUS RISING

The Leo Full Moon lands in your ninth house of belief, Sagittarius, and your perceptions of the world are undoubtedly evolving around this time. Because Pluto is taking up residency in your third house, you're now ready to make major strides in your local community. Notice what themes around travel versus your daily life surfaced back in August last year and ponder what you've learned since that time. Moving, through the physical or astral realms, can be dramatic for you, but that doesn't make it less necessary for your evolution.

CAPRICORN RISING

The Leo Full Moon lands in your eighth house of shared resources, Capricorn, and you're likely to be processing great shifts when it comes to your self-worth and how that's reflected by your bottom line. While you tend to lean on the side of tradition, this lunation is about getting creative when it comes to the support you receive. Don't be afraid to be vulnerable about your heart-felt desires in partnership. The decisions coming to light now reflect lots of promising soul growth, above all else.

HOUSESCOPES

AQUARIUS RISING

The Leo Full Moon lands in your seventh house of committed partnerships, Aquarius, and it's an especially transformational time for your relationships. As you evolve as a person, the people you're committed to will mirror that growth—meaning that people may be making both exits from and entrances to your sphere. Notice the different types of people showing up, and the loud displays they're likely bringing to your life. The most important thing in these interactions is leading with your heart, so if anything is out of alignment with that center, let it leave in peace.

PISCES RISING

The Leo Full Moon lands in your sixth house of wellness, Pisces, and it urges you to examine your relationship between wellness and rest. Luckily, you're no stranger to surfing the astral realm, so this lunation is likely to be an intuitive one for you. What might be more difficult, however, is having boundaries around your immense need for solitude to reach your highest potential. Having company and being a busybody is great, but not at the expense of your health. Notice when your daily life and routines are fueling you, and when they're becoming a drain.

LEO LUNAR FLOW

The Leo Full Moon helps you open your heart to yourself and others. You cannot energetically open your heart if it is physically closed because of a tight chest or back. The body, mind, and emotions all must be aligned for you to feel the magic and radiance of an open heart. The following sequence is designed to help you open your chest and upper back. We often forget that there is access to the heart through both the front and back of the body. The place between your shoulder blades is like a little trap door to the back of your heart. Throughout this practice, focus on breathing into both the front and back of your body, feeling the full circumference of your heart expand.

SUN SALUTATIONS WITH LUNGES: 3 ROUNDS

Begin at the top of your mat. Inhale, lift your arms to the sky, exhale, and fold forward. Inhale, lengthen out your back, and look ahead. Exhale and step your right foot back for a Low Lunge. Place that knee on the ground. On inhale, lift your arms up toward the sky, spending 1 breath here before lowering your hands to the ground and stepping back to Plank Pose. Lower to the ground, then lift your heart for Cobra, keeping your legs on the ground. Exhale into Downward-Facing Dog. Breathe for 5 breaths, then step your right foot forward for a Low Lunge on the other side. Rest your back knee down and, on inhale, lift your arms back up to the sky. On exhale, lower your hands on either side of your foot and step your back foot forward for a fold. On inhale, lift your torso to standing, reaching your arms upward. Exhale, hands to your heart. Repeat this sequence 2 more times, feeling your hips and spine begin to open. On each exhale, feel your abs activate to stabilize your core. On inhale, breathe into your heart.

SUN SALUTATION B/SURYA NAMASKAR B: 3 ROUNDS

Stand at the top of your mat. Inhale, stretch your arms overhead, and bend your knees into Chair Pose. Exhale and fold forward. Inhale, lengthen out your back. Exhale, step into Plank Pose, and lower halfway to chaturanga (elbows into ribs). Inhale and reach your chest up for Upward-Facing Dog, with everything off the ground except your hands and feet. Exhale into Downward-Facing Dog. Inhale and step your left foot forward to Warrior 1, with your back foot flat at a 45° angle. Bend into your front knee and lift your arms to the sky, taking 5 breaths here. Exhale, release into Plank Pose, then lower to chaturanga. Inhale, Upward-Facing Dog. Exhale, Downward-Facing Dog. Repeat on the right side, then remain in Downward-Facing Dog for 5 breaths. Exhale and step to the top of the mat. Inhale, lengthen through your spine. Exhale, fold forward. Inhale, Chair Pose. Exhale, hands to heart. Breathe at the top of your mat as you feel your energy circulating throughout your body.

WARRIOR 1, HUMBLE WARRIOR

From the top of your mat, step your right foot back for Warrior 1. Have your back foot angled at 45° and bend into your front knee. Reach your arms up toward the sky and square your torso to the front of the mat. Feel your heart expand with each inhale and your torso grow taller. Spend 5 breaths here, then clasp your hand behind you, opening your chest. On exhale, fold to the inside of your left leg, keeping your knee bent and hips square to the front. Let your head and neck relax as you look toward your navel. Take 5 deep breaths here, feeling your chest expand and your legs strengthen. On inhale, come upright and step to the top of the mat. Repeat on the other side.

LEO LUNAR FLOW

LOCUST POSE VARIATION: 3 ROUNDS

From the top of the mat, inhale, reach your arms overhead, exhale, and fold forward. Inhale, lengthen out your back, exhale, step back into Plank Pose, and lower to the ground. Lie down on your mat on your belly. Have your legs hips width apart and press into them to create stability in your lower body. Draw your belly in and feel your abs activate to support your spine. Clasp your hands behind your back, opening your chest. On inhale, lift your chest upward into a slight backbend, reaching your arms behind you. Feel as though you are creating traction through your spine as you reach your heart forward. On exhale, lift your legs, keeping them active. Reach your feet and arms back as you expand your chest forward. Take 5 expansive breaths into the back of your heart as you open your spine. Rest in between rounds for 1 breath, then complete the pose two more times.

KING ARTHUR POSE

From your belly, press into Downward-Facing Dog. Step your left foot forward for a Lunge Pose, dropping your back knee. Add padding to your back knee, fully supporting it if needed. Slowly bend your back knee and reach for your foot with your right hand. Pause here. If this is challenging, reach your left arm to the sky and take 5 breaths. If possible, go further by reaching your left arm back, clasping your foot with both hands. Wherever you land, feel your heart reaching toward the ceiling. Breathe fully into the front and back of your heart, allowing the press of your foot in your hand to help you open more deeply. After 5 breaths, release and return to Downward-Facing Dog, then switch sides.

CAMEL POSE: 3 ROUNDS

From Downward-Facing Dog, come up to kneeling with your legs hips width apart. Press down into your shins and activate your abs. Place your hands on your hips with your fingertips going up your back, if possible. Imagine your pelvis pressing against a wall. Keep it there as you inhale to lengthen your spine upward and exhale to slightly bend backward into Camel Pose. Be gentle on your spine and watch your breath. Make it smooth as you deepen the backbend on every exhale. If comfortable for you, release your head back, opening your neck. Spend about 5 breaths here, then come upright slowly. Pause for a moment, then repeat, going deeper the second round.

SPINAL TWIST

Come back down to lying on your back. Hug your left knee into your chest and send it over the right side for a Spinal Twist. Reach your left arm out to the side, stretching through your chest. Take 5 breaths here, then switch sides. On each inhale, feel your back lengthen. On each exhale, twist a little deeper.

SAVASANA

Reach both arms and legs out on the ground. Feel the opening in your heart and the energy from the backbends. Feel the strength in your body as it softens into the ground. Rest here for 5 minutes as your body fully integrates the poses.

FULL MOON MEDITATION

Begin in a seated, upright position with your spine straight. You may also practice the meditation lying down with your body supported by the floor or your bed.

1. Close your eyes and bring your awareness to your heart space—the center of your chest. For about a minute, focus on the beating of your heart. Allow it to calm and focus your mind as you concentrate on the physical heart.

2. Now feel the space around your heart. You may experience it as light, empty space, or an extension of the movements of your heart. Breathe into this space, feeling it expand in three dimensions. Feel the front, sides, and back of your heart. Don't force it to expand in any area; just gently allow your heart space to open with your breath.

3. As you continue to breathe into your heart, feel it expand on the inhale and draw back to the center on the exhale. Feel the rhythm of your breath and your heart merge together in a beautiful dance. Keep your attention on feeling the movement of this space for the next 5 to 10 minutes. If thoughts arise or you start to daydream, bring your awareness back to your heart space. Be curious about what you will find here.

4. While you focus on your heart and breathe space into it, listen to what it has to say. If you experience tension at any point near your heart or anywhere else in your body, tell yourself it's ok to feel. Give your heart permission to express itself, and hold space for yourself to feel. You may experience varying emotions, dreams, memories, or physical sensations, like tingling or heat. Know that these are all just your heart beginning to open and reveal itself to you. Stay focused on your heart space and give it time to unravel. Allow yourself to cry if needed. If emotions become too intense at any point, return to your breath as a point of grounding.

5. Sit with yourself without judgment; there are no right or wrong messages from the heart. There is only the truth. Be open to learning more of your truths. Know that as you experience the layers of your heart, you are making your way to your core essence as a space of love and gratitude.

6. After you've completed 5 to 10 minutes of heart listening, return your focus to the beating of your heart, allowing it to ground you back into the present moment. Feel your feet on the floor, along with the points where your body makes contact with the bed, chair, or floor beneath you. Open your eyes and allow the light to re-enter. Observe how you feel in this moment after spending some time with your heart.

CIRCLE SET UP

This fiery Full Moon in Leo occurs in Aquarius Season. Both Leo and Aquarius are very extroverted signs. They love the company of others. This is a wonderful Full Moon to spend with others to enhance everyone's energy. You can always practice alone, but know that the cosmos is supporting group energy and dynamics this day. If you do practice in a community, surround yourself with people you are comfortable enough to speak freely with about your feelings, your process of release, and your newly formed creations.

CIRCLE SET UP

Choose a quiet location, either inside or outside, to set up your Moon Circle. Incorporate all the elements—especially Fire for Leo and Air for Aquarius. For Air, incorporate auric sprays, feathers to fan smoke from burning herbs, and even wind chimes so you hear the air moving around you. Choose candles to represent Fire, or even build an outside fire. You can use crystals to represent the Earth element. Carnelian, Tiger's Eye, Citrine, and Morganite align with the vibration of Leo. Also, include some crystals to represent Aquarius, as this energy is very much involved tonight. Good choices are Peacock Ore, Goldstone, Kambaba Jasper, and K2. Bring in the element of Water through a room diffuser, a vase with flowers in it, or just a simple metal bowl containing water. Gather all of your supplies and build your circle.

| CARNELIAN | TIGER'S EYE | CITRINE | MORGANITE |

| PEACOCK ORE | GOLDSTONE | KAMBABA JASPER | K2 |

Create an outline with your objects, anchoring the four directions—North, South, East, and West—with either a crystal or candle. If you are creating an altar, set it up in the westerly part of the circle, as this direction gives way for the release of energies. Create enough space for everyone to be comfortable within the circle. Once the perimeter is set, cleanse the area with sage or palo santo. Begin cleansing at the easterly point, moving to the South, West, North, then back to the East. Imagine a white light encasing the circle, protecting it from any external energies. Light your candles and place the rest of your crystals in the circle. Place larger crystals, or a crystal grid, in the center to anchor your circle. Before your guests enter, cleanse each one of them with sage or palo santo, then cleanse yourself. Once you have all entered the circle, pause for a moment to let the energy settle before you begin.

Follow your intuitive guidance when leading a circle. As a guide, begin with all the members introducing themselves. Talk about the astrological energy of the day and how it is affecting each one of you. Share and learn from each other about your unique experiences with this Full Moon. Give plenty of space for each person to speak. Follow your conversation with the meditation practice in this book to calm the mind. You can then explore the rest of the practices. Do them alone, and share as much, or as little, with the rest of the group as you are comfortable with. Go over the questions and continue to learn from each other's perspectives.

Once you're finished with the practices, spend some time in meditation to allow your energy to integrate the work you've just done. Afterward, draw some cards to help tap into your own intuitive guidance. Close the circle by giving gratitude to everyone who chose to honor the Full Moon with you. Give thanks to the elements for supporting you, and to the energy of the Universe for guiding you along the way.

CARD READING

What energy do I need
to hear my heart
more clearly?

+
CARD PULLED:

○

What energy will
help me detach from
my ego?

+
CARD PULLED:

○

What energy will help
me find my true
frequency?

+
CARD PULLED:

○

Reading Cards is a beautiful way to access your intuition and tap into your, and the Universe's, higher wisdom. Anyone can pull cards, as long as you are willing to receive the information they provide. You need no prior experience, or training, just an open and clear mind.

You may use any cards you like for this practice, including but not limited to: Tarot Cards, Animal Medicine Cards, Oracle Cards or any Affirmation Cards. You also can pull cards from a few decks to gain different perspectives. If you are new to card pulling, try to ask only one deck the same question, as asking different decks the same question can become quite confusing. Below are some general guidelines on how to pull cards. Please improvise as needed and above anything else, listen to your intuition.

CLEAR YOUR MIND

A settled, grounded mind is essential for pulling cards. The last thing you want is random thoughts running around when you are trying to receive clear answers from yourself. Practice the breath work and meditation in this workbook to prepare and settle your mind. You may also clear your mind using sound frequencies through singing bowls. These can either be crystal or metal bowls. Play the bowl, or bowls, for about 3-5 minutes to help rid your mind of external noise as you focus on the harmony of the sound.

CARD READING

PICK YOUR DECK
There are many different decks out there. You can choose as many as you like. Know, though, that they each provide you a different energy or medicine. Tarot Cards are the most popular and should be used carefully. Although very useful, Tarot cards can give the wrong impression if you interpret them harshly. Animal Medicine cards offer different types of messages from the animal realm which can help align with the spirit of nature. These cards give you the medicine you need to apply to your situation or question. Affirmation cards provide you with guidance in the form of words or phrases. When reading these cards, it is best to meditate on what the affirmation means for you. It is also helpful to repeat the affirmation a few times and see how it makes you feel. There are many other cards you can experiment with, like Goddess Cards, Angel Cards, and so on. The important thing to remember with any card is that they each have different angles and sides. There are often a few interpretations of the same card.

SHUFFLE
Shuffle the cards the easiest way for you. Some cards are smaller and can be shuffled like a regular deck of playing cards, while others with take some effort. If all else fails, spread them out on the floor in front of you then regather them. Keep a clear mind while shuffling. You can also repeat " I am open to receiving guidance and intuition." Refrain from asking your questions until the next step.

LEO CARD QUESTIONS
You are free to ask the deck any questions you need answers to on this Full Moon. The following questions are meant to help you harness the energy of Leo through the cards to clarify some of these energies in your mind. This is a three-part card reading, where you'll ask the deck three questions. Before beginning, spread your freshly shuffled cards in a wide arc in front of you. Use your left middle finger to choose the card, first waving your hand slowly over the cards. You'll feel a magnetic pull, or slight tingle, in your fingertip when you hover over the right card. Chose one card at a time, taking a moment to breathe in between questions. Keep the cards flipped over until you pull all three.

What energy do I need to hear my heart more clearly?

What energy will help me detach from my ego?

What energy will help me find my true frequency?

TAKE THEM IN
Once you have your cards, flip them over. Before looking up their meaning, sit with them for a moment and allow them to speak to you. Intuit your own meaning and interpretation of the card. What is the card trying to tell you? What are you trying to tell yourself? After a few moments with the cards, look up their meaning. Sit with that information, merging it with your intuitive meaning of the cards.

As with everything, enjoy this process. Do not worry if you are doing it right or wrong. Just follow your intuition, and trust the journey. Accept the cards you are dealt and use their energy wisely to help guide you when you need it the most.

She no longer feared the fires of her life
instead, she walked right through them

- spirit daughter

LEO PRACTICES

This Full Moon allows us to become aware of where we are aligning with the ego and detaching from the infinite love of our hearts. It shows us how we have disconnected from the frequency of love and instead are vibrating with lower energies, like judgment, shame, fear, and guilt. This Full Moon can also illuminate when we allow anger and resentment to take over, blocking the heart's work. It also reveals how we seek to separate ourselves from others to validate our existence or make us feel uniquely talented in some way.

The first step of the work this Full Moon gives us is to look at how you misalign your energy with your heart. This can be a challenging step, but it's important to look at how you may be ignoring your heart to align with your ego or how you think you "should" be. We often create an identity around ourselves that fits in with some image of who we think we need to be in the world. This image may help get us what we need. It may help us feel good about ourselves or offer a platform for judging others.

While the ego can serve us in identifying ourselves among the collective, it always needs to be kept in alignment with the heart. For instance, the ego can help us create labels for ourselves that describe personality, work, and even relationship status—labels like "I'm a Leo," or "I'm a nurse," or "I'm single." Once we start using these labels to judge others or to feel better, or lesser, than our peers, we become misaligned with our hearts. We have allowed the ego to take over. The ego seeks to define, which can be good, but it's important to remember that we can be different from others while still being of equal value on all levels. Everyone is unique in their own way, but no one is more unique or more special than anyone else. Both Leo and Aquarius remind us of this. They teach us to honor and love all beings for who they are in this world. When we look at the world through the lens of the heart, it becomes easy to balance the ego and see the interconnected beauty of all beings.

1. What definitions of your ego are you attached to? How do these attachments block your heart's guidance?

_____

_____

_____

_____

_____

_____

_____

_____

_____

_____

LEO PRACTICES

2. What are three things you have not accepted about yourself because your ego has made you feel you weren't supposed to embody these things?

_____

_____

_____

_____

_____

_____

_____

_____

_____

_____

_____

_____

_____

3. What would you be able to release if you lived from your heart and felt interconnected with all beings?

_____

_____

_____

_____

_____

_____

_____

LEO PRACTICES

_____

_____

_____

_____

_____

The ego, although useful, limits us. It limits our hearts and our capacity to love. It makes us feel we need to put conditions on our love for others and ourselves. It tells us how we should feel and act, and what we need to achieve. If we don't do those things, the ego makes us feel unworthy of love from others. The ego will rule our lives if we let it, and it will end up making us feel unhappy, unfulfilled, and not good enough. Love is what helps us leave the limitations of the ego and journey to the higher Self. When we align with love and compassion, we align with who we really are—the person beyond the confines of the ego. We see ourselves in our entirety and understand the path we are on this lifetime. We let go of all the ways we "should" ourselves into thinking things, and instead we embrace the life of the heart.

Breaking through the limitations of the ego can be challenging, as we've been taught much of our lives to align with it. However, you can start on this Full Moon to balance your ego with love and feel your unlimited energetic potential.

4. What are some ways your ego makes you feel unloved or unworthy of love? Are these true, or are these just tricks of the ego?

_____

_____

_____

_____

_____

_____

_____

_____

_____

_____

LEO PRACTICES

_____

_____
_____
_____
_____
_____
_____

5. How does it feel to think you can be free of the ego and let go of all the things you "should" do and instead just be?

_____
_____
_____
_____
_____
_____
_____
_____
_____
_____
_____
_____
_____
_____
_____

LEO PRACTICES

Staying in the frequency of love asks that you see yourself in everyone. It asks that you see the interconnectedness of all beings and have compassion instead of judgment. Every day we can choose how we interact with the world. When we live from the higher Self, we show up with an open heart, even if it makes us feel vulnerable. We see the uniqueness in everyone we meet, and we love other beings unconditionally. Even if we don't agree with others or they trigger us, we understand they are made of the same energy that we and the rest of the Universe are made of. They deserve compassion, and they are just as unique as everyone else. Living in this vibration of love requires a commitment to our hearts. It doesn't mean we won't fight for justice or that we'll gloss over every wrongdoing. It means that we will fight from love and do everything—including help right the world's wrongdoings—from a place of love. This power can be found in the highest integration of Leo and Aquarian energies. Feel the frequency of love on this Full Moon, and commit yourself to it.

6. Do you feel vulnerable when opening your heart to others and acting from the vibration of love?

_____

_____

_____

_____

_____

_____

_____

_____

_____

_____

_____

_____

_____

_____

LEO PRACTICES

7. What helps you calm this vulnerability, embrace it, and see it as a strength to signal that you are on the right path?

_____

_____

_____

_____

_____

_____

_____

_____

_____

_____

_____

_____

_____

_____

8. What helps you remain in the vibration of love? What commitment can you make to yourself to help you return there when you have lost your way?

_____

_____

_____

_____

_____

_____

LEO PRACTICES

_____

_____

_____

_____

_____

_____

_____

9. How does it feel to live through your heart and see yourself in all beings?

_____

_____

_____

_____

_____

_____

_____

_____

_____

_____

_____

_____

_____

_____

_____

_____

LAST QUARTER IN SCORPIO

FEBRUARY 2ND

We are halfway between the Full and New Moons, a time of clearing and magic. The Last Quarter Moon represents the final stage of the lunar cycle. It is the time to completely shift the energies you don't want to carry into the next lunar cycle. With the Sun still in Aquarius, the Moon lands exactly 90° today, creating a square aspect and our Last Quarter Moon. Squares cause friction in the energetic body, but they give us the opportunity for a breakthrough. With Aquarius and Scorpio contributing their energy to this Last Quarter Moon, we have the opportunity to break through any fear of our shadows and step into our authentic truth.

Scorpio is the fearless magician of the zodiac. She is guided by her intuition alone as she traverses the unknown. She bravely dives into the depths of her own subconscious to discover the truth of her own existence. Along this journey, she learns that everything, including herself, is made of the same substance: energy. Through this understanding, she gains the power of transmutation.

Align with the energy of the Moon and Scorpio today to transform energies that are blocking you from showing your true self to others. Courageously peer into your subconscious layers and find pieces that you keep hidden, even from yourself. Give them compassion and attention as you bring them out of the darkness and into the light, where they can be transformed.

Scorpio gives us the power to take the energies and emotions that weigh us down and turn them into something that helps us reach new heights. Take your anger or frustration, and turn it into motivation. Shift your anxiety into excitement. Find creativity and beauty among your sadness and depression. And, if you feel brave enough, perform the greatest alchemy and turn your deepest fears into trust. Scorpio reminds us this Moon that we create our reality and can create any frequency we want to live among. It just takes a little magic.

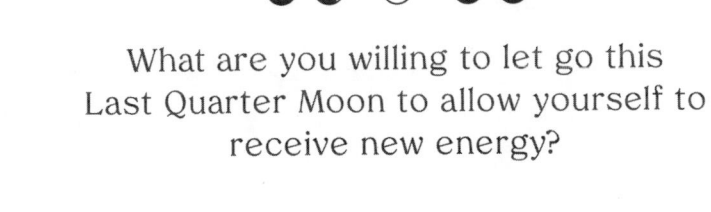

What are you willing to let go this Last Quarter Moon to allow yourself to receive new energy?

AFFIRMATIONS

Think of people in your life or the world who embody their authentic truth. Write down some words to describe them and their qualities. Also, feel into what it would feel like to step into your full Self. Write down words that describe this feeling. What does your energy feel like? What do you emit into the world from your truth? Collect as many words as you can to describe yourself and others living their authentic truth.

_____

_____

_____

_____

_____

_____

_____

_____

Now create 3-5 affirmations that use the words listed above. Write powerful "I am" statements that help you tell the Universe how you want to feel each day and the energy you are ready to receive.

_____

_____

_____

_____

_____

_____

_____

_____

_____

_____

_____

HAPPY
FULL MOON!

Thank you to everyone who supported and purchased this workbook.

Special Thanks to Rebecca Reitz (rebeccareitz.com, @becca_reitz) for her beautiful artwork on the cover & pages 2, 4, 6, 10, 13, 16, 30.

For a monthly subscription contact hello@spiritdaughter.com or visit www.spiritdaughter.com.

Disclaimer: The exercises and yoga sequences in this book are physical activities that should be performed carefully to avoid injury. You agree to accept all risks and release Spirit Daughter and any guest instructors from any and all liabilities. Please take care and enjoy.

Follow along our journey on IG:
@spiritdaughter

We always love seeing your photos & hearing about your experiences with the workbooks! Tag us to be featured on our community page:
@spiritdaughtercollective

For more information contact:
hello@spiritdaughter.com.

First paperback edition December 2023

Book design by Rebecca Reitz
Cover design by Rebecca Reitz

ISBN 978-1-960013-48-4 (paperback)

www.spiritdaughter.com